Anam,
You are amazing!
my wish for you is that
you connect with the
lessons in the book.

Love,
Saira

To all those hurting:

I see you.
I hear you.
I am sorry.
I forgive you.
I release you.
I send you love, light
and healing.

Simply Saira

...and so she
RISES

simply saira

PR: the QRATORS

Editor: Sara Gustafson

Cover Design: Maham Momin

Photography: Joseph Chander Photography

Interior design: Lazar Kackarovski

ISBN: 978-1-9994953-4-3

Published by Simply Saira.
www.simplysaira.com

Your struggles, tears, and heart-ache
paved the rocky path.
You did what you knew best
given any circumstances
and that is to love unconditionally.

You loved your family,
neighbours, friends, enemies
and oppressors alike.

They shattered our glass houses
and you smiled while picking up
the pieces every single time.

You built and rebuilt our lives
over and over again.
Your strength, courage and
resilience is remarkable.

You held us in our weakest.
Loved us through our worst.
Encouraged us through the
toughest times of our lives.

Thank you for walking this path
before us and for being
a role model of love and courage.

Thank you for inspiring us
to do better and be better.

Thank you mom

CONTENTS

Contents

Contents

Contents

The Rise... 179

Contents

The Woman...

WHO IS SHE?

I am the woman
that many men laid
their eyes on to feast.

I am the woman
that overcame
abuse and
sexual harassment.

I am the woman
that beat death.

I am the woman
that defied all odds
to create a new reality
for her life.

I am the woman
that has been aching
to be heard.

I am the woman
that is breaking her silence
to encourage other women
to take control of their lives.

There is no other day like today
and there is no time like now
to rise up and leave
all the adversity behind.

It is time to become the woman
you were always meant to be
and to take control of your life.

HER ROLES

I am a friend, sister,
daughter, and a mother.
I am a Pakistani Canadian.
Above all I am a woman,
and a human being with emotions.

I am not your elevator to success.
Nor your free ticket to Canada.
I am not your typical Pakistani girl,
whom you can mold to conform
to your made-up customs
and religious ideals.

I say the F word,
I cuss and I speak up.
Most importantly,
I have learned to forgive.

I do not seek vengeance
I am better than that.
I choose different
and that is what sets me apart.
I choose compassion
even for those who do not wish me well.

I have no time for haters.
But I do believe in Karma.
So hang in there,
my wounds will return as theirs.

BECOMING SIMPLY SAIRA

I repeatedly got knocked down
because I tried to be somebody
for everybody.

Until I realized,
that I did not need to be anything
for anyone, but myself.

I needed to love me,
accept me,
embrace me,
embody me and
fully trust me
for me.

I needed to become
simply myself
for me.

This has been
one of the most
profound revelations,
which led me towards
myself.

This is how I became
simply myself.
I became Simply Saira.

And that is
more than enough
for me.

My wish for you
is that you gather the courage
to simply become yourself
for you.

The Love...

UNIVERSE

You are the center
of this wonderful universe.
and your soul
is a beautiful companion.

SPECIAL MOMENTS

Lifetimes move through us
in the blink of an eye.
What feels like a lifetime of love,
can be summed up into
a few special moments.

ON ITS WAY

The love that is meant for you
will find its way to you,
as soon as you are ready
to receive it.

FLAWED

It was time
to bring down the walls.
He wanted it bare and raw.
The hurt, the pain, and desires.
The successes and the failures.

Each scar had a story to share.
Some were real and
some were false.
It was too shameful
to have him see the truth.

So I was told,
no man is man enough
to love a woman who is flawed.

FIRE

They had a fire
burning equally.
His warm touch
sent shivers
down her spine
till the very last day.

She craved his warmth
and her craved her cool.
They were irresistible.
Total opposites and
inseparable.

Yet incompatible
and incomplete.

GROWTH

Lucky are the souls
who grow together,
become better and
create a memorable
future together.

NOT EVERYONE

Your capacity to love
is expansive
but not everyone
is made for the ocean.

NIGHTS

Some nights we spent
tangled into each other.
Your warm body pressed
against mine.

Those were my favourite
nights.

EXPRESSION

Whisper good night
and express your love
as she drifts into deep sleep.
Because she holds onto
these moments
while she sleeps.

You will have her
fall in love with you
all over again
every single night.

It is these small moments
that make the world
of a difference
for her and
her inner world.

BE IN LOVE

Be in love
but do not strip
others of their rights.

Love does not equal
control over mind, body
or soul.

Fear-based love
and attachment
is a result of manipulation
and abuse.

Stand up
for your rights.

TRUE LOVE

If he truly loves you
and you love him
his focus and intention
will be to treat you
like his queen,
and for you to treat
him like your king.

Do not imprison each other
in a relationship that could
take years to escape.

PERFECT BLEND

All the things I love in you,
are qualities that no one else
possesses.

These are unique to you
because they stemmed
from my desires.

You are the perfect blend
of a dream
and a cruel reality.

Your true essence is love,
and that makes you
my favorite forever.

LIKE THE OCEAN

His love was like the ocean
ready to take me.
I preferred to swim
on the side-lines
in the shallow waters.
Fear of the unknown
scared me a whole lot.

Huge waves of his love
came to take me in deeper.
I never liked the deep end,
I could not stay afloat.
I grasped for air.
It was too much to handle,
I nearly drowned.

He saw my pain
and struggle.
The waves pushed me
onto the shore,
then waited for me
to catch my breath.
Gave me a comforting hand
and returned to the depths
of the ocean.

I waited on the sidelines.
I promised to learn
how to swim.
I promised to take care of us
and our love.
It was too late.
The sun had already set
and the darkness
had taken over.

I WANT US

I want you
whole and complete.
I want us
every day of our lives.
I want to savor every moment
with you.

You breathe life into me.
My life force.
My love.
I want to live
a life beyond limitations
where time is infinite
and lovers dance in eternal love.

SLEEPING TOGETHER

We slept together
many times
before marriage
without physical touch or
a sexual desire.
I would watch him
transition into deep sleep
on my laptop.

That innocent smile
while mumbling my name
in his sleep,
was more than enough
to melt my heart
and swell my eyes
with tears.

I praised God
every single time
for the amazing man in my life.

BEING HEARD

Being heard is such a beautiful feeling,
especially when it is from
the one you love.

IT EXISTS

The best kind of love
is knowing that it always existed
between the two of you
but you never knew it
until you found each other.

BE A VESSEL

They envied our love.
They were confused and hurt
by not being adored the way I was.
They saw how lovingly I was treated.
They saw how much he cared.

They refused to understand
that in order to receive love
you need to give love.
In order to be adored
past the honey-moon phase
you need to adore in return.
Anything that you desire to receive
you need to give that to yourself
and others first without any expectation
or disappointment.

Allow yourself to be a vessel
of infinite love and respect
not just for your spouses or
favourite siblings but for everyone
who enters your experience.

DREAMS

He can read me like a book.
He can see through my love,
heartache and pain.
He knows the right things to say
that bring me the most comfort.
His presence reassures me
that dreams do come true.

PHONE

I did not hear
the phone ring, he said.
Funny, because I do not need
a loud ringtone to know
that he is calling or
sending me a message.

I never really needed
a notification to know that
he wants to get in touch with me.
My heart accurately
notifies me 99.9% of the time.

PAIN

Pain often trumps and conceals
the love that we have staring
right into our eyes.

We disregard it
as we work through
and process our pain.

The Betrayal...

THE BATON

The baton of pain,
betrayal and heartache
is passed down for generations.

It is suppressed, ignored
and accepted as the norm
by many men and women
of all ages, races and religions.

Until they decide
that enough is enough.
Decide to break the baton,
and dismantle
these painful cycles.

PRAYER

He prayed for a woman
whose body was pure,
and they raped her soul.

ISOLATION

I was sentenced to isolation
for a crime I did not commit.
I was innocent yet proven guilty.
He was the life force for me,
yet too blind to see the truth.

They said I was not a good wife,
a good mother, or a good woman.
I did not deserve
to have him in my life.
They said I was worthless
and I believed them.

MASTER MANIPULATOR

She wore the mask of a friend
and an empath.
She burned with envy,
and ached with hate.

It was like two sides of a coin.
Two different personalities
active at all times.

One was fake
for the world to see
while the inside was real
for God to see.

Her vibes did not lie.
She was creative and captivating
with her words and emotions.

She was a wolf,
that acted like a sheep.
She was the master of her craft,
a master manipulator.

She preyed on those she envied.
Lucky for me, she envied me for decades.
It is her hobby and she enjoys it much
as she searches for new victims daily.

Identify her.
Listen to your intuition.
Protect yourself from master manipulators,
both male and females.

DELUSIONAL

I raised my voiced once again
against the injustice,
the lies and deception,
and once again I was pulled
by my hair and thrown out of his life
through harsh words
to silence me into submission.

I know what I saw,
I know what I heard,
and I know what I experienced
but still they claim that I am delusional.
They say that I am making up stories
to cover up my lies, deception
and tracks.

There is no one who can testify
in my favour.
God is the witness of my truth
and I need him with me
more than anyone else today.
Who else could I turn to?
Where else could I go
to be loved, accepted and trusted?

SELF REJECTION

You rejected me
because I was rejecting myself.

You did not want me in your life
because I did not want to live.

You abandoned me
because I fully abandoned myself.

SHADOWS

Some nights he just waited
for me to fall asleep
so that he could disappear
in the shadows.

You see,
he loved being in the darkness.

TERRORIZED

She says I caused her divorce
but no one knows
the truth of what transpired
behind closed doors.

If the walls could speak
they would scream of the horror
she caused in our home.

If the doors could testify
they would tear up
in the pain we experienced
while living in so much fear
and abuse, only to save
my brother's marriage
and his son's life.

If the empty spaces could be filled
they would carry our pain and tears
from days, weeks, months and years
causing massive floods in the city.

The sad reality of it all
is that no one cared to validate
her lies.
She continued to terrorize us
in our home,
and those who claimed to love us
believed every single word of hate
that she spread around the city.

OLD AND WISE

Open your legs
and let me tell you
all about my wedding night.

My wife was not a virgin,
I wasn't loyal either, he said

He began the tale with such pride.
I used to have my way with women.
I was a desirable hunk, he said.

She threatened to yell for help.
No one would believe you, fool.
I am old and rusted, he said.

It was just a game you see,
he wanted to have his way with her.
Promise not to tell,
and we both keep our dignity, he said.

As the tale goes,
she was silenced yet by another man,
who was old and wise.

TOO FAR

Not this time!
This time
you have gone too far.

This time you played
with my child's heart.

She deserves better.
She deserves more.

She will embrace happiness.
She will be at peace.

Don't you worry darling.
She will learn to forgive.
She will conquer life.

WOLF AND THE SHEEP

When the wolf
finally fell for the sheep.
He let her in
to see his vulnerability.

Blinded by his words
she would never have
known true love.

Her mind and body
deserved more respect
than his need for authority.

It took months
to transition into intimacy
and that terrified him

The wolf felt emotions
he could not process,
while the sheep carried his breed.

Terrified and confused
the wolf repeatedly attacked
and ran from the sheep
who magnetized a change in him.

Change can be scary
and uncomfortable,
it can either bring out the best
in you or the worst.

WALKED OUT

He walked out
when I needed him the most.
It was by far one of the most
traumatic experiences.

How do you even begin
to articulate losing someone
you love so deeply
that you breathe
every single breath for them.

His walking out
helped me stand up
and walk on my own feet.
Miracles do happen
and this was both
a miracle and a blessing
in disguise.

DO NOT HOLD BACK

They continue to attack
with burning rage
and in fear of losing control
over your mind and life.

These types of people rejoice
in isolating and weakening your soul.

You, my love are not weak.
Let them see the incredible strength
that you have within.

Now is not the time
to hold back.

WALLS

The walls
you build around you,
the little girl in me
tries to climb daily.

She falls.
She hurts.
She fails.
She cries.

And she gets back up
to fight with herself daily.

ACCUSATION

Where did you go
with him
and why?
These questions
tore my soul apart.

My lover, guide, protector,
and my soul mate
lost his trust in me
following accusations
from his sister.

He stepped away
in agreement with the accusers
when I needed him the most.
In a battle of love and hate,
love lost its fate and purity.

I felt poisoned,
left to suffer minute by minute.
But I did not perform adultery.
It is not in my character to cheat.
I thought he knew that.
I thought he knew me.

We were in the war zone
and everywhere I turned
landmines embraced me,
I do not recall accepting
this call to war.

I have seen many like this before.
Men and women alike
feeling threatened by my presence.
What is it that they see in me,
that I do not?

How do I cease fire?
How do I tell them
that I mean no harm.
They actually believe
that I am capable of winning
their beloved brother's heart
for him to follow me
to the ends of this planet.

Why could I
not have the same belief?
They see someone in me
that I do not.

Someone who is capable
of rocking the boat,
causing their entire foundation
built on lies
to collapse.

Someone so incredibly strong,
and powerful enough to lead
the pack.

MARRIED TO FAMILY

I cannot seem to understand
who I married,
whether it is you
or your family.
It has been two years
since we last lived together
I have been holding on since.
I have been waiting
to see your promises
be fulfilled and to live a life
alongside you and our daughter.

Your love, presence, trust
and commitment
is all I ever wanted.
You have failed to give
our marriage the basic pillars
that hold a marriage together.
I do not know how much
longer I can hold on
in the midst of the chaos
that your family continues to create.

I do not know how much longer
I can hope to receive the love and respect,
which you have not yet provided.
Our religion allows for a woman
to receive and be so much more
in a marriage that I have been stripped of.
Islam allows for a woman
to give to her husband so much
that you have restricted me from.

I do not know how much longer
I can continue to live
with this guilt and self-hate
that stems from the treatment
that I have allowed you
and your family to give me.
I do not know how much longer
I can continue to accept
the blame that is not mine.

Please forgive me
if I can no longer hold on.

THE OTHER WOMAN

I never imagined
there would be another woman
in our marriage.
Someone who is consistently
weakening our bond,
while competing for his attention.
She has made every attempt
to tear us apart.

She wins every time
because she is family.
I lose because even after
giving our marriage 100%
I am treated as an outsider.

It is a perfect example
of hate, envy and
women tearing down
other women.
She continues to live her life
alongside her husband and kids
while I live as a single mother
and my girl as an orphan.

WEB OF LIES

We were both lied to.
we were both manipulated
by those we trusted.
We never wanted
to let each other go
but the web of lies
was too powerful to escape.

Our love caved.
It could not withstand
the hate projected onto us.
We separated
but still held onto
that love in our soul.

INCAPABLE

I felt incapable
of raising my daughter
and protecting her
like a father ever could.
This society and culture's ideals
have sucked every ounce
of confidence and belief
out of me.

I spent hours daily and weekly
crying at my misery.
From the time she was born
I begged him to stay.
I begged him for his presence
because I repeatedly felt incapable
of protecting and caring
for the two of us.

REPEAT

Someone who pushes
you out of their life
will not hesitate to do it
over and over and over again.

DECEPTION

She wanted to see me suffer.
She said, she could not wait
for my death.
I uncovered her lies
and proved her wrong to our family
whom she deceived for years.

She led with lies,
and she led with hate.
She believed in divide and conquer.
She tore our family apart
to create her kingdom and rejoiced
in doing so.

I brought my family back together.
Removed hatred from their hearts,
and spread love and light.
She could not bear to see
her rule come to an end.
So she ventured out
and continued to spread hate, lies,
and deception in the community.

ONE MORE TIME

It was always
one more chance
for me, for our daughter,
just one more time.

I never stopped giving
him yet another chance and
he never stopped giving
me excuses.

YOUR SISTERS

You are ready to jump
at men who raise their
voices at your sisters.

Your wife is also a sister,
mother and daughter,
whom you treat so recklessly.
Islamic rights equally apply
to all women.

STILL SEARCHING

She let go
parts of herself
for him and his love.

Even then,
she was not enough.
Her purity was not enough.
He always searched for more.

DEATH

Death knew
I was eternally yours,
or was I?

CONTRACTUAL MARRIAGE

I could not give them
what they wanted in time.
If I had known the price
for your love, trust, commitment,
and companionship needed
to be paid up front, and to them
I would never have engaged
in a contractual marriage.

No contracts were signed
yet my desire to live with you
was seen as breach of contract.

INFLUENCE

Accusations, name calling
lack of trust and hatred
is what I received
during the darker days.
But I still stayed.

I kept going back,
because I saw how much love
he was capable of giving
when he was not under
anyone's influence.

CHEATING

The man who cheats
in a relationship
also has the ability
to be loyal.
The difference
is in your belief
about what you deserve.

HIS VOICE

First he raised his voice
then he spoke a bit louder
then he yelled
and went on a rampage.

Every instance of this rampage
sucked the life out of me,
leaving my body shaky
and voice jittery.

The more he raged
the weaker I felt,
emotionally, mentally
and physically.

The Fall...

HER DARKNESS

He loved her light,
her angelic face
that gorgeous smile
lustrous lips
big brown eyes
long luscious hair
her sexy body
and the way she stepped
into all her glory.

When the darkness fell
her light diminished
taking with it
her angelic glow
and the gorgeous smile.
Her happiness transformed
into unexplainable sadness.
From all her glory
she fell flat to the ground,
completely numbed,
unable to feel emotions.

Seeing her bad, ugly
and painful demeanor,
he pushed her further into it
and ran because he only
wanted the good and
the beauty.

BACK AGAIN

They may come back
in your life
sweep you off your feet
and lead you to believe
that this time it will be different.
This time it will be better.

Then they stomp all over you
reminding you why you left
in the first place.

EMPTY

Congratulations!
You have emptied out her soul.
She will now confine to cultural
norms.

She might attempt to shine again.
She may not fit into a box yet.
Go on. Strike again,
for the darkness to spread inside her.

You are doing great.
Suck the light out of her,
she is almost there.

Her light will not
be diminished forever.
She will rise.
You'll see.

REGRET

Was it fear, guilt or pain?
I longed to have you speak.

Your fear broke me down,
ripped my heart open,
and I could not breathe.

I wish I had walked away
before you caused me pain.

YOUR WOUNDS

I searched your eyes for the truth
that your mouth could not speak.

I waited for the moments to help you heal
from the wounds that were so deep.

My soul could not see you cry
in the darkest hours of the night.

LOST

I was lost
in the desires of the world.
The rat race
and the successes.

While God was planning
a temporary home for me
in the holy city of Makkah,
just meters away from salvation.

We can dream up our dreams
and make grand plans for our lives,
but God's dreams and plans
are always bigger and greater
than we can ever imagine.

SHAKEN

My soul
has been shaken awake,
yet my body is numb.

Could this really be?
Am I actually
in the holy city of Makkah?

Did God really love me
or is this all a dream?

I did not spend years
in worship.
I ask myself,
as I stand before God
confused, hurt, shaken,
and shattered.

ROCK BOTTOM

After falling for so long,
hitting the ground
has finally given me hope.
There is nothing
deeper and darker
than rock bottom.

This may be the hardest fall,
but I am here now.
No one else to pull me up.
Just you and me,
for as long as you desire.

I am open
and I am all ears.
I am ready for my lesson.
Speak through me
right here,
right now.

BEAUTY IN DARKNESS

The beauty of Rock Bottom
is that you get to develop
a strong relationship with
yourself and God.

You get to un-learn and re-learn
anything and everything
you desire.

It is where you get to build
a solid foundation for your life
exactly how you desire.

It is where your will and
God's will unite.
It is where you get to become
UNSTOPPABLE!

JOURNEY

I walked for miles to reach you.
My feet sore with blisters
and my toes covered in sand.
I arrived only to know
that I did not arrive.

You were never my destination
only a short lay-over.
I must take the scenic route now
to savor every moment that follows
as my beautiful journey
toward life continues.

NOT READY

I search for you daily
as I try to make sense of it all.
Your promises, gifts,
the love and those memories,
I still carry within me.

Loving you completes me.
Letting you go
is tearing my soul apart.

SHORT-LIVED

Every time you tried to return
you gave me hope.
I felt alive again
for a few short moments.

My soul knew
we could not reside together.
The flowers knew
your stay was short-lived.
They refused to bloom with me.

The universal signs.
The fierce rain-drops.
The dead leaves.
The vicious waves of the ocean
did not change course
whether you stayed or left.

I refused to believe their whispers.
I refused to believe my soul.
Every time you managed
to pull the life out of me
for a few short moments.

FALSE LIFE

I have lived many lies
to honor the wishes
of those who loved me.

Some lies were excruciating.
Some peeled off
many layers of my skin
to reveal the raw, vulnerable
 and the weakest in me.

The twinkle in my eyes
dimmed over time.
The reflection in the mirror
was no longer mine.

I lost all facets of my existence
my truths, and my desires.
To live the lies of those
who once claimed to love me.

IDOLS

She put them on pedestal.
Idolized them.
Protected them.

The idols
could not withstand the storm.
They crashed and broke
into a million pieces before her.

God reminded her.
How fast idols can rise
and fall.

After all,
they are simply human
just like the rest of them.

PRECIOUS HOURS

In the moments
that my heart ached for him.
He was in prayer
asking God for me.

I picked up the phone
a few times but feared rejection.
There was a battle inside of me
of what ifs and why nots.

He spent many precious hours
of the night in prayer for me
and I for him.

STILL WAITING

I have been standing
where you left me.

I will be right here dreaming
up a better life.

Because today's reality
is too painful to accept.

CHILLS

I have had chills
for a few days.
My body is suffering
in a battle between
the heart and mind.

Heart wants to feel
the emotions
but the mind
wants to numb them.

I am just a spectator
watching from afar.
My body is refusing
to take control.
We are just waiting
for the battle to end,
so that my suffering
can ease off.

GOD'S SPEED

Have you ever seen
two parallel train tracks meeting?

Well, the heaven conspired our union,
then tore us apart.

It is disastrous to remain attached
to that which is toxic.

Heaven moves fast at God's speed,
while it may take us years to catch up.

UNWANTED

We both thought
the other did not want us.
Feelings of not being wanted
are fatal especially
because it takes
all that you have got
to give all that you are
to that special someone.

LET HIM GO

Every single man
that you will attract
after your husband
will be the exactly like him,
she said.

Am I cursed, I asked.

No. You need to forgive, she said.

Why did he come in my life,
if he was not meant to stay?
I asked, as I broke down in tears.

He came to show you
that you were empty inside.
It was never about him.
It is about you,
and what you do
with this experience.

Let him go, she said.

I can't, I said.

You must go on, she said
as her timer beeped
and our session concluded.

Here I am two years later,
still holding on
hoping, praying and wishing
for my miracle.

SEPARATED

Many attempt to connect
when they learn
I am "Separated".
I can fulfill your needs,
some say
while others
call my husband a fool.

Just give me a chance
and I'll make you
the happiest woman alive.
Or, you are gorgeous
beyond belief
I can do anything for you.

I am drowning
in this frustration.
Sexual desires
may be of importance
but my relationship
with Allah
is of higher value.

I reject such offers
because I do not seek
pleasure outside
of a marriage.

I am just not that
type of a girl.

I WANT ME

Return all of my love,
my tears,
sleepless nights,
my words of comfort,
happiness and
all of that which I had given
you so willingly.

I want all of me whole and complete
who I was when I was truly me,
before you tore me into someone,
I am not.

STAY AWAKE

Do not close your eyes,
try to focus,
pay attention and
stay awake just a while longer.
It will all be over soon.

The tiny voice whispered
in my head.

TRAUMA

You have experienced trauma.
Why do you keep reliving the past?
asked my therapist

I have been lining up the events
and memories as they occurred.
I wanted to make sure
what I saw and felt actually happened
because they deny it, I said.

You are not crazy Saira.
You are NOT crazy.
If you believe it to be true
then it did happen,
she said.

THERAPIST

It felt like I was losing my mind.
I was beginning to believe them
and question myself.

I once again was allowing
external sources to control
my inside world.

Sometimes it can take someone
neutral to bring you back
and keep you in check.

In my case it has been
my coach, my therapist.

FORGIVENESS

Have you forgiven him?
she asked.

Yes I think so,
I replied.

No, you have not.
Your body language and energy
tells me otherwise,
she said.

I nodded,
as I lowered my head.

LIVES INSIDE ME

He was never my EX.
It always feels strange
referring to him as my ex.

He has been a lot more to me
than just a shadow
from my past.

He continues to live
inside of me
year after year.

FITTING IN

I feel like I do not fit in.
I feel like I do not belong
in this world.

I do things differently.
I desire the simplest things.
I do not enjoy gossips.
I do not indulge in hatred.
I do not want revenge.

I feel like I do not fit into
the norms of this society
where envy, self-hate, racism
revenge and hatred thrive.

I look around me and
wait for a peace-filled reality
to take form.

It is being shaped
in my inner world.

I can feel it
I can breathe it
and smell it
but have not touched
nor tasted it yet.

OVER AND OVER

It takes an incredible
amount of courage
to lose the one you love.

But it takes a ridiculous
amount of courage
and resilience
to lose the same person
over and over
and over again.

THE HARASSMENT

From the first day we met
he showed that he cared.
He expressed his approval
of our marriage.
He raved about my beauty
and how lucky my husband was.

I was grateful to have
another elder brother who cared.
He always sat across from me.
Discomfort crept in as
he began gawking with his wife
by his side.
The extended handshakes
were of no brother.
I mean I am all for admiration
but only from my husband.
I thought it was a phase.
I thought he would stop.

He made an effort
to be in family photos
while standing next to me.
His camera followed me
at an event that day,
while his wife carried their child.
He criticized his wife for being too big
as he praised me for my slim figure
with my husband by my side.
I thought it was a phase.
I thought he would stop.

I stayed at their house
because it was expected of me.
But I could not last a week.
The gawking never stopped
nor did the discomfort.
I thought it was a phase.
I thought he would stop.
While leaving my mom's home
that night, he held my hand
in a long and uncomfortable handshake.
He caressed the back of my hand
while piercing through my soul.
He undressed me
and raped my soul
in a few short moments
with his eyes.
I thought it was a phase.
I thought he would stop.

I cried for days.
I tried to shake off the dirt.
I took extended showers daily.
I wrapped up my body better
with a hijab.
My soul could not be cleansed.
The dirt never washed off.
I thought it was a phase.
I thought he would stop.

We circled around
as grandma showed off his new-born.
He was beaming with happiness
and gawked from across the room.
He made his way toward me
while giving hugs
to every single person in his path.
I froze at his sight.
I prayed for invisibility.
I prayed for my shield.
The dirt he rubbed on me
was thicker this time.
I thought it was a phase.
I thought he would stop.

He stood closer and closer
to me that day.
He stood behind me for picture time.
His elbows rubbed on my back
as he carefully photographed
the entire family pack.
I thought it was a phase.
I thought he would stop.

He observed my body from
head to toe in the hospital bed this time
with my new-born in his arms.
He compared my body to his wife's
with the entire family by his side.
I fixed the blanket over me,
I hid my feet in.
But the dirt kept piling up.
I thought it was a phase.
I thought he would stop.

I spoke up two years too late.
He was disguised as someone
who cared for the praise.
I was the one to blame.
I was the one at fault.
No one did believe,
no one came to my aid.

I thought it was a phase.
I thought it would pass.

He became the reason
my character was tarnished,
a painful memory I suppressed.
I did not speak of it again.
I had long forgotten.
So much time had passed.
So many memories have faded.
But that day, when the cashier
touched my hand,
he did not mean any harm
yet it triggered a memory inside me.
I felt dirty.
I tried to shake off the dirt.
I thought it was a phase.
I thought it would pass.

I could not remember
why my hands felt so dirty.
I could not remember
why the dirt would not wash off.
My mind suppressed the trauma
that was now waiting to explode
to allow the healing to unfold.
I allowed my body time.
It took over a year
for the memory to resurface.
I thought it was a phase.
I thought it would pass.

I am now able to articulate.
I am now able to remember.
I now have the capacity to forgive
because I believe it was not my fault.
It was a phase that persisted
because I allowed it to happen.
It is all in the past now and
it will not repeat.
My soul will heal.
My soul will find home.

EMOTIONLESS

Some days
I just do not know
how to feel.
I have a hard time
processing my feelings
and emotions.

The day my body
experiences a shock
I feel heavy emotions
to the point of excruciating pain
and then my body shuts down.
I become emotionless.

I may appear calm
and collected on the outside
unaffected by the chaos
around me.

But on the inside
I am hollow.
I am empty.
I am drained.
It is like the storm inside
of me ceases into a drought.

This is the aftermath
of repeatedly experiencing trauma
and not being healed from it.

NIGHTMARES

What do your nightmares
look like, he asked.

They are either chaotic,
with a lot commotion, police
and ambulances
or they are quiet and suffocating
with a shadow pressing a pillow
against my face. - I replied

They are quiet disturbing
and traumatizing.
It is like reliving the excruciating
pain over and over again
every single night.

UNATTACHED TO MONEY

Sitting here, staring
into my bank account
with the last $1000 left in my savings
from my corporate days.
I protected and held onto this money
that I had worked so hard for.

I see visions on a daily basis
to donate and let it all go.
I cannot seem to gather myself
to donate the last bit of money
I have left.

I am neck deep in debt
and I have no idea where
more money will come from
to buy milk and diapers.
I have zero confidence left
to carry out conversations.
How will I go out into the world
and make a living again?

God please do not make
me do this, I need this money.
I plead, as I sob into my hand
for hours in the darkest hours
of the night.

It needed to be done.
I needed to learn to unattach.
I needed to learn to let go
and trust in the higher source.
For once I was grateful
to have a roof above my head,
to have food on the table
and be surrounded by a caring family.

NO BROWNIE POINTS

A man that is incapable
of making decisions on his own
when it comes to his wife and kids
feeds off of the joy of pleasing
someone else other than Allah.

There are no brownie points
for being an obedient son
or an obedient brother
if he is incapable of treating
his wife right and
being a present father.

SPECIAL PLACE

I lied to myself
that I did not need
him in my life.
I wanted to move on
for the better.

I appear calm
on the outside
but there is still a void
in my heart.
A special space that
I cannot allot to anyone else.
It belongs to him.

MEET HIMSELF

The one you are waiting for
has yet to meet himself.

NO MORE HIDING

Avoidance
does not help
you move further
neither does hiding.
Whatever it is
that you are avoiding
or hiding from,
you need to face it
head on.

WINGS

He promised to take care of her
because he loved her so
She was precious.
He cut her wings
and put her in a beautiful cage.
She broke down,
and could no longer fly.

BEYOND TIME

We set sail,
to a land beyond time.

It exists.
My heart knows it does.

That is where you live.

BATTLES WON

I fought the toughest battles
when no one would fight for me.

I was asked to back down
because no one wanted to stand up for me.

I was knocked down, dragged, humiliated,
and crushed on the fields.

I lost my courage and desire to get back up
then HE reached down to lift me up.

The battles that I fought over and over
were already won for me.

YOUR HOME

Your home was in my heart.
They tore a piece of my heart out
when they pulled you away.
They do not realize the degree of pain
they chose for themselves
in this lifetime.

Home-wreckers
rarely find peace within.

UNANSWERED

Some prayers are better
left unanswered.
I am alive today because
my plea to embrace
death was not fulfilled.

The Healing...

WHAT IF

What if
there is a bigger picture here.

What if
there is love, healing and
beautiful opportunities that
await you.

Beyond all the hurt, pain,
struggle and obstacles.

What if
you just need to forgive yourself
and others.

What if
you simply surrendered
to God's will.

Yes
it can be that simple.

Open your eyes baby girl,
to see what God sees in you,
and for you.

What if
everything is for your highest good.

What if...

SURRENDER

Sometimes you need
to cry it out
in order to let all your hurt,
pain and fears flow out of you.

Allow yourself to break
in the hands of God,
and only God.

Put it all on the table before him
and ask for guidance.
Surrender as you ask
for the love and support you desire.

Then sit back and feel the warmth
in which he embraces you.
Feel your body being cleansed
of all the negativity, hurt and pain.

Allow the seeds of hope
and positivity to be planted in your heart
then visualize with conviction the life
you truly desire and trust
in it fruition.

DIVINE LIGHT

You will heal
when it is time for you
to heal.
Not when others
expect you to heal.

Continue to rise up love,
and know that the darkness
is leaving you.
The divine light
has been on its quest to you.

Let her in.
Simply let her in love.

HEALING

Your healing is sacred.
It is your own journey,
your path to walk and discover.
No rule book.
No guidelines.

Sit with yourself and
listen to what your mind, body,
and soul need to heal.
Give yourself time.
Healing will come.

ANXIETY

Dear Anxiety,
I am breaking up with you!

You held me back,
led me toward self-doubt and criticism.
You shattered my self-confidence,
and led me toward insomnia.

You visited and revisited over
the last few years.
But this time around,
you shook me down to the core.

Stripped me to reveal
my inner deepest scars,
fears, and most importantly
my most precious passions.

I went into hiding because of you.
I went on an inward journey,
and faced all that boiled inside of me.

After months of self-discovery,
you helped me uncover
and pursue my true passions.

You helped me realize
that it is ok to create
an outrageous vision for my life.

You taught me how to surrender
to the almighty whole-heartedly
and without guilt.

Heck, you taught me
how to truly practice unattachment.
Although you brought me
down to my knees,
you led me toward
a more meaningful life.

Anxiety, I'm breaking up with you,
not out of hate
but out of love.

You served me well
and this time more so
because I welcomed the lessons.

I understand now
why you revisited all these years.

And now it is time for me to up level,
and continue to apply the lessons learned.

I wish you well,
and release you with love.

Dear Anxiety,
I am breaking up with you.

BLOOM

Your love is like a drug
that can get anyone intoxicated
but causes havoc in the body.

God took you away
because it was not our time yet.
I will wait for a new sun to rise
for the flowers to bloom again
and for my heart to heal.

My love belongs to someone
who deserves it.
Someone who is grateful
to share his life with me
every single day.

ANOTHER LIKE ME

Go on
search high and low.
You will not find
another like me.

My inner world
is ever expanding.
The wounds and scars
are healing.

Your presence,
love and lust can lead
many to self-destruct.

Hold on tight darling,
as you lead yourself
to self-destruct,
in search of another
just like me.

KNIFE

Put the knife down
you have done this once
but not this time.
This time you are not weak.
This time you know better.
This time you cannot allow
your emotions to cloud your mind.

You have a beautiful life
waiting for you.
You can get through this.
The relationship
was never meant to be.
Its failure does not define you.
It has helped you grow stronger.

You can choose to continue
to heal your wounds
and not wound yourself further.
Hurting your body
is a form of self-rejection
when you need to be the one
to accept yourself.

You need to be the one
to love yourself in every way
that you expect from others.
You need to be the one
to embrace, forgive and heal yourself.
Only you know what you need
to come out of this stronger than ever.
Give yourself that.
And be gentle with yourself.

TOUGH

It is not always easy.
Developing inner strength
is hard work.

Waking up every morning
and fighting past memories
is tough.

Self-soothing and self loving
especially when guilt leads
to self-hate, is challenging.

Standing strong every day
to fight for a beautiful future
takes immense courage.

Staying stuck in the same memories
and habits is the easy part.
Choosing different and better
takes every cell of your body
to say ENOUGH.

Let's vow to ourselves
to choose new,
different and better every day
because enough is enough.

BROKEN DREAMS

As you ponder on your broken dreams
and goals you could not accomplish.
The passions you left behind because
they felt none of it was good enough.

How is it not Muslim of you
to be a woman, sister, daughter or a mother
and have passions, goals, and dreams?
Why could they not bear to see you shine?

They feared to have you break
the glass ceiling,
which they once dreamed to reach,
and failed.

They validated their own fears
by holding you back.
Those dreams, goals, and passions,
which they also once had.

Do not hate them for the pain they caused.
Deep inside they are also hurt, broken,
shattered and flawed.

Send them your love,
compassion and forgiveness.
For what they did
had also been done to them.

It is time for you to let go,
rise up and dream again.
The dreams, goals, and passions,
are all waiting for you.
Let's break that glass ceiling baby.
It's time.

CONTEMPLATING

I spent many nights,
thinking, wondering
and contemplating
my words and expressions.

How? Why? But...

Many questions surface,
as words swim
across my notebook daily.
They take a life of their own
as if they are searching
for a new home.

Self-doubt and
negative inner voices
become louder than ever.
The outside world
becomes much more dominant
than the inside world.

I question myself
as if I already expect
to be questioned.
I pick myself up and
run through
this fog of confusion.

I remind myself that
I am meant to be here.
My words are powerful
and so are my memories,
The pain, the hurt and
my experiences.

They deserve a new home.
They deserve to be seen and
they deserve to be heard.

SAND-CASTLES

People may run from you
because they attract
a challenge in you
that they are not ready for.

You challenge their beliefs,
stories, actions and
thought processes.

Your mere presence
makes them feel threatened
in their own skin.

When you thrive
you challenge their ideals
that they have built
their sandcastles on for generations
only to have them crumble.

GREATNESS

They attack you.
Try to break you.
And then run from you
because they aren't ready
to break their negative cycles
and patterns.

When you challenge one
you challenge generations.
Their entire family legacy
and the honor and pride of those
who came before them.

Know that they aren't
running from you.
They simply are not ready for
the challenges you
bring to the table.
They are comfortable
where they are at,
so leave them there.

And Run.
Because YOU are meant
for bigger and better.
You are built for greatness.

PURITY

The soul and your body
are not enemies
they are your allies
pure as the fresh rain-drops
falling from heavens
and as clean to carry
the fragrance of jasmine
for lifetimes after lifetimes.

MEMORIES

The memories
you are holding onto
are safe to be left behind.

The past scenarios
you play and replay
in your mind
are not real.

Life happened
exactly it was meant to.
Embrace yourself
and your present.

It is only uphill from here.

IT IS POSSIBLE

It is possible to be kind
with yourself and others
after being broken.

It is possible to put yourself
back together and
forgive those who hurt you.

It is possible to fall in love
with yourself and life again.

There is always dawn after darkness.
Your broken pieces
can become your greatest strengths.

Follow your inner voice,
your heart's truest desires
and everything becomes possible.

NEW REALITY

The things that you strive to achieve,
yet do not pursue within yourself.

You expect miracles of God,
yet disregard the miracles within you.

Everything you expect of life
you already are.

Step forward and embrace
your higher self.

Your new reality
awaits you.

REFUEL

Look at yourself in the eyes,
and say I Love You.
Give yourself a hug.
Take yourself out on a date.

Watch the sunset.
Go for a long walk by the water.
Watch your favourite movie
and dance to your favourite tune.

Do what feels good to you
to refresh, refuel and re-energize.
Go ahead spoil yourself,
because you deserve nothing less.

BEAUTIFUL CONNECTION

They said
you will never return.
I trust we will meet
in another lifetime.

Our souls share
a beautiful connection.
That will live
beyond lifetimes.

STEP FORWARD

I tried.
I judged.

I reasoned with myself.
I made a list of why
and why not.

Still,
I could not get myself
to hate you.

My love for you
is pure.

And I left,
because I needed
to love myself.

INNER BATTLE

Some days are a battle within.
Some days I am ready to give up.

And some days I remind myself
why I am walking this path
to begin with.

Then some days
are the brightest and happiest ever.
Those days carry
my favourite moments.

NOT THE RIGHT ONE

It is not that you were wrong.
He just was not right for you.
Do not question your self-worth.

He did not deserve to be in your life.
This experience, this heart-ache
might just be another pattern
that you need to break.

You life is filled with reminders.
It is time to step it up and
take control of your own life.
It is time to step into the woman
you were destined to be.

Allow this experience
to be your last fall
and toward your highest rise.
You deserve the best.
Do not ever forget that.

I AM COMPLETE

I began to hate,
the parts you hated of me.
It was easier to love
certain aspects within each other.

We never became whole
nor accepted one another as complete.
I tried to let those parts of me go,
but instead I lost myself.

If it is a prerequisite to be broken
in order to earn your love
then I choose to keep myself
as the whole being,
and let you go.
Because I am whole.
I am complete.

YOU ARE WORTHY

They know you are worthy.
They have always known.

But do you know your worth?
What will it take for you
to accept your true worth
and deserve ability?

You are worthy.
You are so loved.
You deserve all the happiness,
abundance and freedom
that your heart desires.

HIS MEMORIES

Some days his memories surround me
wanting to reunite with every cell of my being.
They remind me of my strength and resilience.

His memories are a distraction,
a gentle reminder of the amount of love
I still carry within me.

Moving on is not about hate.
It is about choosing and loving
me every single day.

I FEEL IT

I can feel it
every time he thinks of me.
I can hear his heart beating
inside of me.
The fragrance of his skin
is oh so fresh around me.

I can feel his pain,
his struggles, and heart-ache.
He left a piece of his heart
inside of me.
I cannot seem to dig it out.
We share a strong connection.
That is my gift and a curse.

BETTER VERSION

Reliving the past
has not served you yet
so why would it now?

You have
a greater purpose to fulfill.
You have transformed
into a better version of you.

Do not walk down
the same old path.
Those roads only lead to
self-destruction.

Those people and memories
are no longer yours.
Let them go
on their own path.

You have your own destiny to live.
New doors are opening for you.
Just knock.

RAINBOWS

Look for rainbows in your clouds.
Sadness may seem like forever
but it is not permanent.

Happiness is inevitable
and also a choice.
And you are free to choose.

BE ENOUGH FOR YOU

Just because
you were not enough
for that one person,
does not mean
you cannot be enough
for yourself.

Do not allow
external sources
to diminish
your sense of worthiness

You are Enough.
You are Worthy.

DO NOT RUN BACK

When you ask the higher sources
for a better life and you continue
to be cracked open,
hold your ground.

Do not run back
to what caused you
the most pain and trauma
before healing can come.

FOCUS ON ACTIONS

When you are done
crying for someone
who was never yours
to begin with.

Know that if he wanted
to spend his life with you
he would have never
walked away.

Focus on his actions
not empty promises.

DIVORCE

If you want a divorce
then pray for my death
instead, he said.
He meant every word of
"till death do us apart"
in our union.

I felt like a captive
completely blinded by my emotions
to see the pain behind his words.

I can see everything clearly now.
The fog has been lifted
and the sun is shining so bright.
I can see beauty miles away from me
and in ways that I could never see before.

"Till death do us apart"
was also my wish in our union.

SHINE

If you have been
cracked open
do not conceal
or hide from it.
Forgive yourself
and allow your truth
to shine through.

APOLOGY

The apology,
you are waiting for
has been there all along.
Look within
and forgive yourself.

STAND STRONG

You expect others
to do for you
what you do not have
the courage to do for yourself,
only to be disappointed
over and over again.

You can stop this cycle.
Only you can give yourself
what others failed to give you.
Give yourself whatever it is
that your mind, body and soul needs
every single day.

Stand strong in your truth
and reclaim your power now.

CONNECTED SOULS

Our souls are connected
like the connection between
a mother and the baby in her womb.

If this is true
then my thoughts are yours
and yours are mine.
My emotions are yours
and yours are mine.

To bring forth change,
I simply need to change
my thoughts, emotions,
and perspectives
to have them reflect in you.

I realize now
we are all mirrors of each other.
Reflecting back our deepest fears,
thoughts, emotions and beliefs
to each other.

REASONS

I looked for all the reasons
why he would not stay
and so he did not stay.

I waited for him to return,
but he was long gone.

I forgave all the reasons
that caused him to drift away

I let go.
I surrendered.
I became unattached.

And focused on
my well-being instead.

THE SOURCE

Their presence in your life
does not define your self-worth.
Your sense of self-worth
determines their presence in your life.

Your self-worth,
and what you believe you deserve
is reflected by the people in your life
and your life experiences.

Believe you are valuable,
and treat yourself
how you expect to be treated.

Believe that you deserve
the best that life has to offer,
and give yourself daily reminders
to shift your belief system into it.

You are the source of it all.
You get to decide
what you will and will not
allow in your life.

CHOOSE AGAIN

If I had to choose again
I would choose you in every life-time.
Not because our love is eternal
but because losing you strengthens me,
time after time.

I elevate to new levels of courage
every single time.
When I feel like
I have been stretched too thin,
I surpass a new level of feeling alive.

I love you for your role in my life.
Although, heart-wrenching,
it is exactly what I need to elevate.
The light that follows the storm
is so much more beautiful.

I would choose you
time and time again as the storm
because I love the beauty
of nature after the storm passes.

THE ONE

If he is not
the right one for me
then I do not know what is.

Every day I prayed for him
to become the best
that he could be.
For me. For us.

Did he become it?
Is he the one?
Only time will tell.

PERMISSION

You are putting your life on hold,
for someone who continues to live
his life to the fullest.

You are putting your passions on hold,
for someone who passionately engages
with that he loves.

You are putting your goals on hold,
for someone whose goals
do not include you.

You are putting yourself on hold,
for someone who continues to flow
like the ocean,
taking with him everything
that appears on his path.

You are the one at a loss here love
not them.
It is time to give yourself permission,
to start living your life again.

VIBES

You cannot make up vibes.
Your body language
eyes and facial expressions
speak louder
and clearer
way before your words.

PRIORITIES

Sometimes your peace of mind
is a lot more valuable
than your need to be right.

It is ok to desire to be heard
but how others receive
your words and message
should not be your concern.

Your priority must be you,
your well-being
and your peace of mind.

PARALYSIS

There is so much peace
in this state of unconsciousness.
They all think that I will make it
but they do not realize that
I feel paralyzed.
I am unable to move
with my free will.

This is the state
those before me spoke of.
The place where death embraces you.
After being rejected for so long
death sees me as worthy.
I do not know whether to be
overjoyed to finally feel accepted
by a force far greater than me
or be devastated to not be able
to see my family again.

The angel of death has arrived
to take me with him.
But instead he gives me an option
to either use the gateway to depart
or stay on planet earth.
Of course I wanted to go
but my soul decided to stay.

My soul chose life,
so I can see my princess again.
She did not ask to be in this mess.
She deserves a better reality
and now we will create it.
In a matter of seconds,
a healing energy entered my body.
It flowed from my toes to my hips,
upper body and my head.

I am now able to open my eyes,
wiggle my toes, move my fingers
and lift my arms.
In a matter of minutes,
my paralysis has healed.
I have never felt so close to God
as I did in these moments.
I never imagined that
this state of unconsciousness
can bring so much peace and wisdom.

When my conscious mind
took over, it was chaotic.
There were still so many lessons
left to learn.
I needed to master a new level
of calmness and peace.

ACCEPTANCE

The world will not be ready
for your honesty and purity.
They will always see you
as flawed until
you fully accept you.

PASSIVE SUBMISSION

You broke me
far too many times,
far more than I deserved.
Your love hurts
so I wonder if it really is love.

My self-expression
is unacceptable to you.
Because you desire
passive submission.
These are qualities that
I do not possess.

Will you continue
to punish me until I submit?
Passive submission
is no longer in my bones.
Try and punish me
as you please but
I will not waiver.

IDENTITY

I chose to keep
my last name after marriage.
In a culture where
women are not only expected
to leave their family behind
but also cut ties with them,
giving up their last names
is also highly expected and
pushed upon them.

My refusal to do so
was a big shock to their egos.
I was pressured to give up
my identity like the ones before me.
I fought and stood by my decision
because I learned that
it was cultural expectation and
it had nothing to do with Islam.

When my religion allows
me the freedom to hold onto
my identity then
other people's egos
are none of my business.

ABUSERS

You can either let
the voices of the abusers
become loud enough
to over-power your inside voice
or you could decide to stay
grounded in your truth
and cleanse the clutter
out of your life.

Drowning out the voices
that are not yours to keep
is a huge step forward
and so incredibly empowering.

SELF-LOVE

To fall in love with your-self
so deeply and passionately
that you see the beauty
inside of you regardless
of how much darkness
surrounds you.

To fall in love with yourself
is a true privilege
and you do not need
to wait an eternity
to meet yourself
and fall in love.

Stand up right now,
and introduce yourself
to you in the mirror.
You are everything
you have been waiting for
and more

MEANT TO BE

They cannot keep
us apart for long.
The souls that are meant
to be together
will find their way
back to each other.

THE BOY

The boy will always
push you out of his life.
Do not be fooled
by his looks and age.

A man that is broken
at heart is forever a boy.
And boys do not have the capacity
to stand up for themselves
and will never stand up for you.
You have to stand up for you.

RUMORS

I waited for the day
when she would
finally speak the truth
and all the rumors would disappear.

I later realized
how much value I assigned
to someone outside of myself.

LOOK WITHIN

You are not restricted by time,
place or the people you are with
to pause, reflect and take a moment
to connect and realign with yourself
and God.

Look within, that is where
the magic begins.

KNOTS

Some knots are beyond
your ability to unravel.
Reconsider where you
choose to invest
your emotional energy.

Nurture your inner child.
Invest your beautiful energy
in you.

TRUST

When it feels like
you are not being trusted.
Look within and reflect
where in your life
are you not trusting
your inner voice.

SOOTHE YOUR SOUL

When your friends turn against you.
The entire community sees you at fault.
The world becomes too small
for you to seek refuge in or
you begin to believe
the accusations forced upon you,
know this, that there is a greater being
above it all.

When you have no where to turn,
no shoulder to cry on,
no one else to soothe your wounds,
no one to embrace you
or provide comfort to your soul,
turn to God.
Turn to that divine power
that you whole-heartedly believe in.

Allow him to provide you
comfort and soothe your soul.
Allow him to wipe away your tears.
Allow him to lift you up
and open new doors that you never
imagined existed.

You never have to prove
your innocence nor your truth to him.
He is the all-knowing.
The most merciful.
And the one who loves you
the most.

HEAL AND LET GO

What does it even mean
to allow your mind and body
to heal itself?

Healing comes from allowing
yourself to feel all of the emotions
that come through you.

Imagine yourself as a gateway
for these flood of emotions
to find a safe passage
and be released.

Anytime you suppress
the emotions due to guilt, shame,
embarrassment, resentments or regret
you block the gateway.

Emotions that cannot be felt
and are suppressed
block you from your own happiness.

Years of blocks can make that
your body's default
and instead of feeling,
you automatically numb the pain.

Allow your body to do
whatever it needs
to get the flow going.

There is no right or wrong.
You can move from numbing,
to anger, to forgiving
and letting go.

Key is to learn and grow
from the experience
and let it go.

JOURNEY INWARD

It is not about
what he said or she said.
It is what you say to yourself
that matters and
what you allow into you.

It is not important to
put your trust into the world
that has previously let you down
but putting your trust into yourself
that makes the world of a difference.

It is not necessary to withdraw
from those who claim to love you
but bringing your focus and
attention toward nurturing you.

It is of the highest good
to tune into you, your needs
and desires and to come home
inward to yourself.

BOUNDARIES

May we understand them.
May we create them.
May we honor them.
May we speak our truths and
May we protect our mind,
body and soul.

WEIGHT

When you put down
the weight of the world,
that is when you will finally soar.
Let that shit go love.

REPEAT LESSONS

There are no mistakes in life,
only lessons.
Some lessons you might
need to learn from
more than once.
And that's ok,
because it is what you need
to strengthen yourself.

The Rise...

BOOK OF LIFE

Stop looking back.
You have turned these pages
far too many times.
You have memorized
these chapters
and all the chapters
leading up to it.

Your book of life
must go on.

Pick up that pen
and allow your desires
to flow freely on the pages.
You have the power
to write the new chapters
with your truth.

No one can take this
away from you.
You own it.
It is yours.
Pick up that pen
and take your power back.

THANK YOU

Thank you for the heart-ache.
Thank you for not trusting me.
Thank you for pushing me away
over and over again.

Because of you...
I have learned to heal my heart.
I have learned to trust me.
I have learned to stand up for me.

Thank you for all the lessons.

STORM

The sky
is not falling apart.
The storm has passed.
Your world
is piecing back together.
Allow it
and trust it.

PACT

Let's make a pact
together you and me,
to not chase the shadows
that have drifted away from us.

To not mourn those
no longer a part of our lives
not because they left
but because they saw our worth
way before we did.

That terrified them
to know that we deserved
so much more than
what was presented to us
given our circumstances.

The Future YOU –
so much more radiant, worthy,
fearless, courageous and inspirational
is waiting for the present YOU.

Why wait?

I AM ENOUGH

I am so incredibly enough.
Always have been.
There is nothing left to prove.

I know and believe this truth
as I stand in my power with grace.
The higher source supports me
in everything I do.

Because
I AM so incredibly enough.
And so are YOU.

SIGN FROM UNIVERSE

You asked the universe for a sign,
and then you received the perfect sign,
or was it always there.

We see what we are meant to see,
in every given moment.
Not more, not less.

Your cry and call to the universe
is answered every single time,
and that time is deemed perfect for you.

Your next assignment
and your next miracle is on its way.
Everything is right on time.
Hang in there.

CRACKED

I finally cracked
after years of silence.
Love that I had buried away
has erupted.
There is no
stopping it now.

TAKE CHARGE

You will always be
as happy as you decide to be.

Decide,
and be in charge
of your own happiness.

MOUNTAIN

Once you reach the top of the mountain
there is another one waiting for you.
Slightly bigger and a harder climb.

You get to rediscover yourself.
Your strengths and weaknesses,
successes and failures all over again.

You have the capacity and will-power
to push beyond your present self
into a renewed, strengthened
and recharged self.

FOCUS ON ME

It felt like I had been failing
at this thing called life
with no purpose.
I was pushing hard
in the wrong direction.
I had it all wrong.

I needed to focus on me.
build me up,
love on me and
fill my own cup.
When I had nothing
left to lose,
I finally followed and
pursued my passions.

One step at a time
one decision at a time
I gave myself all the time
in the world.

WALK AWAY

It becomes easier and easier
for you to walk away
from those who disrupt
your inner peace.

The manipulators,
the controllers,
and the ones with hidden agendas
show up every now and then.

The heightened level of awareness
that you developed and carry
can smell them from a mile away.

Your tendency to attract
these types of people
is not your weakness.

With proper boundaries in place
once they show you
who they really are,
walk away.

No regrets.
No attachments.
Value yourself enough
to protect your inner peace.

Turning your weakness
into strengths and super-powers
can be so incredibly liberating.

HELL AND BACK

I have been through Hell,
and came out stronger than ever.
You did not break me darling.
You do not own
that kind of power over me.
I am the one in the driver seat
with God as my GPS.
Always have been.

Own your power.
Step into your shining light.
Be your own knight.
Your dreams are waiting for you.

BUILD A DOOR

Walk away from closed doors
that do not wish to open for you.

The cracks in the windows allow
for the sun to shine through
yet they remain shut.

Build yourself a door
where you see a ray of light
and walk right through it.

Because when opportunity
comes knocking
you need to be able to open
the door to embrace it.

Open the door.
Embrace the new you,
and live your life
as your heart desires.

NO MORE REGRETS

When all is said and done,
I can look back and know
that I did everything
I possibly could to save
a broken marriage, and
mend my shattered heart.

Sure, there are a million things
I could have done differently.
These are all lessons not regrets.
I did everything in my control
knowing what I knew then.
Things that were beyond my control
were all dealt with by God.

No more regrets now
and no more tears.

REALIZATION

Those blinded
by the lies
rarely find happiness
in accepting the truth.

DECISIONS

I have lost one too many battles.
I have grieved you.
I mourned you as my biggest loss.
I will not mourn again.

I have suffered one too many times.
I will not allow you
to become my biggest sorrow.

Either you are in
or you are out.
I have decided.
Have you?

I AM HOME

I collected,
shoes, handbags, clothes, jewellery,
and many expensive things.

Owning them
did not increase my self-worth.

Hitting rock bottom
taught me my true value.

Now I collect memories
and many special moments
one day at a time.

These precious moments
make me feel like
I am finally at home with myself.

NOT YOUR PIT STOP

You see value in me
more than I could ever see.
My vision had been tainted
by the lack of worthiness
drilled in me.

You clearly see the value,
and that keeps you wanting
to come back to me.

I see the pattern though,
you are not here to stay,
but rather to refill your cup,
and walk away.

I am not your pit stop
or a refueling station.
If you valued me enough
you would have honored me
in every way.

I have learned to honor me,
in ways that others could not.
So the door that I had kept open
is now closed.

INDULGE IN SELF-CARE

There is nothing sexier
than a woman who honors
her soul and
indulges in self-care
daily.

WAVES

Emotions
flow through me like
an infinite amount of waves.

Each carry a message
some blessings
and some gifts.

SEA

My view is infinite beauty
I do not want this to end.

The beautiful sounds
are on an infinity loop.
The water gives me life.

Like a mermaid
I wish to unite and
sleep beneath the beautiful
sea tonight.

VALUE YOUR WORDS

Some words
need not be told,
nor heard,
nor spoken,
they need to be felt
with your soul.
Those words
move mountains.

Leave them astounded
and speechless.
You owe nothing
and they deserve
no explanation.
Your words
will move mountains.

QUEEN

Take my hand and
lead me on a beautiful journey
toward love, compassion,
fulfillment and beauty.

Allow me to feel
your love, strength and passion
in the depths of my soul.

Hold on tight
to my dreams this time,
the thieves
stroll the streets daily.

Experience the joys
of life with me
and through me.

I want to spend
every second of my being
united with you.

Hold my gaze darling,
as I express my infinite love,
admiration and compassion
for you.

Saira, I love you!
You are My Queen.
I am my own Queen.

My love, admiration
and respect for myself
grows immensely every single day.

FULFILL YOUR DESTINY

No one can make decisions
for you better than YOU.
No one can comfort, soothe
and take care of you,
the way you can.

God has already decided
what the utmost best is for you.
It is up to you to step into it
and claim your destiny.

No one else can live that for you,
only you can fulfill your destiny.

VOICE

May our voice comfort
those who need to hear it.

May our voice encourage
those who have been crushed.

May our voice inspire
those who need to rise
above adversity.

May our voice empower
others to do great
in the world starting with
themselves.

No one should ever
have to live in abuse, fear,
depression or lack.

We all deserve to create
and live our best lives.

SUPER-POWER

I will no longer allow
anyone to disrespect me
or treat me like I am
worthless,
while they expect me
to believe that I did
everything to deserve
this treatment.

I will no longer allow
anyone to project
their fears and
insecurities onto me,
while they expect me
to believe that their
words and behaviours
are justified.

No one has the right
to walk all over me
and if you do
then you do not
belong in my life.
These clear boundaries
are my super-power.

PERCEPTION

It does not matter
what people think
or say about you.

What matters is
how you perceive yourself.
Do not allow
the opinions of others
to cloud your perception
of yourself.

God sees you as worthy,
honest, pure, and
pretty darn remarkable.
You have nothing
left to prove.

Treat yourself
with immense love and respect.
Those who matter
will mirror it back to you
and all else will fall into place.

I promise.

MY WISH

Do not spread hate and pain
so graciously.
When it comes back to you
because it will,
only then you will realize
why no one is around to pull you up.

My wish for you is that you find
the peace and healing within
that your soul so desperately needs
only then will you reconsider
hurting another Saira.

LET THEM GO

Some people may not choose
to be in our lives while some
do not belong in our lives.
Either way, send them love
and let them go.

HELL OF A FORCE

My desires
are erupting out of me
like a volcano.
The fireworks have begun.

The crowd
of those who broke me,
have gathered.

These fools do not know
that my will and God's will
have united.

I am not the one they broke.
I am a hell of a force,
with God's will
bestowed upon me.

PHOENIX

You could crumble,
hit rock bottom
and burn to ashes
over and over again,
and still have the ability
to rebuild yourself,
grow stronger,
and rise above it all.

You are a phoenix at heart.
You have the ability
to fly high with grace
and reach the destinations
your heart desires.

You are a phoenix at heart.

VALIDATION

You were created
by the divine with a purpose.
Hence no further validation
from anyone is necessary.
You already are everything
you need to be.

EXPANSION

What if you do not need
to replace the love you carry within,
with someone else's name?

Your capacity to love
can only expand not shrink.
Each name can carry
its own weight and space
in your ever-expanding
universe of love.

Embrace the expansion.

YOU ARE ALLOWED

You are allowed to change
your decisions.
You are allowed to start over.
You are allowed to choose
the best outcomes for you.
You are allowed to move away
from the situations that are draining.
You are allowed to leave
unhealthy relationships behind.
You are allowed to choose you
and be the best that you can be
for you.

I AM READY

I am ready to let you go.
I am ready to set myself free.
I am ready to send you love.
I am ready to embrace
the freedom-filled life that I crave
where I get to decide the experiences
that I want to have,
the people that I want to align with
and the learning that I want to choose
for my highest good.

I am ready to let you go.
I am ready to set myself free.
I am ready to send you love.

TIME

Time has a wonderful way
of showing us
what really matters
in our lives.
Invest your time wisely.

CLOSURE

The stars lined up once again tonight.
They whispered your name,
this time they asked why I no longer
mention your name.
Many have asked of you lately.
With every attempt they make
to dig into my wounds,
I smile and walk away.

This is what closure feels like
on my side of the world.

ALWAYS

You will always be in my heart
and I can always speak to you
on a soul level,
beyond this chaos of the world.

CHAMPION

I did not get here overnight.
It took years of courage
to pick up my broken pieces
and face my inner demons
in order to rise above adversity.

If you are reading this
and feel like you are not
further ahead than you were
yesterday, last week, or last month,
please know that I honor you
for recognizing your desire for progress.

They key to continue rising
is to acknowledge the progress
you have made so far,
love yourself even more
and release any self judgement.

Celebrate your wins, my love.
You are a champion.

The Author...

ABOUT THE AUTHOR

Simply Saira is a Pakistani-Canadian author, speaker and coach. She came to Canada at the age of 11 and found herself bonding with art and writing as a form of self-expression. Coming from an immigrant family she has been passionate about creating a better life and a different future for herself and her family.

Saira excelled at all levels of her education earning various awards and scholarships from College and University. She started her career at the age 21 and very quickly worked her way up in the company. She was at the peak of her career, working and studying in Project Management, at the time of her marriage and made a tough decision to leave her career behind in order to start her married life.

Not too long after getting married, she found herself living in the midst of abuse and hit rock bottom. Since then, she has invested thousands of dollars in her personal development to learn, grow, heal, and expand in order to rebuild her life alongside her young daughter.

Saira started writing again during some of the darkest times of her life as an avenue to allow herself to express her deepest emotions and heal from the trauma. She has emerged as an inspiration for men and women around the globe as a strong and compassionate woman. She truly embodies grace and strength and empowers others to be true to themselves. Her words always carry gifts in the form of encouragement for everyone.

Saira is on a mission to inspire, encourage, coach, and empower others to rise above adversity in their life and to fall in love with themselves all over again, because no one should ever have to live in fear, hate, lack, depression or abuse.

CONNECT

@iamsimplysaira

@iamsimplysaira

@iamsimplysaira

www.andsosherises.com
www.simplysaira.com

hello@andsosherises.com
hello@simplysaira.com

CPSIA information can be obtained
at www.ICGtesting.com
Printed in the USA
LVHW010404111118
596689LV00003B/3/P